This book is dedicated to the love of my life Gaby. There is no way this book could have been completed without your support, inspiration and all-around goodness.

Much appreciation to my son and buddy Lee. Your playful insights have shown me the way many times.

Secrets of a
Creative Warrior

A Practical Guide for Developing
Your Creative Confidence

••••••••••••

Seth B. Greenwald

Published by LookinGood Publishing
Pleasantville, NY
www.CreativeWarriorSecrets.com

Printed in the United States of America
First edition: January 2013
Updated: September 2018

ISBN 978-0-9886827-0-2
Library of Congress Control Number: 2012922854

1. Creativity   2. Personal Growth   3. Success

Table of Contents   Page

Part Two: Techniques to Inspire Creativity

Foreword

When I was a kid I wanted to fly. So I did. I extended my arms, took a small leap off my bed and soared over my hometown on Long Island. My red cape flapped excitedly behind me like a badge of courage.

At school I wanted to maintain that superhero mindset. So I did. Hard test? No problem! I'd connect with my awesome powers and wham…instant 100%. Of course, I had x-ray vision and didn't need to crack open any books to study. Yes!

Ahh, those were the days. As school progressed I was taught to rely less on my imagination and more on my all-important intellect. Thinking, they said, is king and the ruler of our destiny.

But what if it isn't? What if our creative superhero is still within us, just waiting for our call? What if all we need to do to reconnect with it is to become aware of the thoughts which hold us back from trying exciting new things? What if all it takes is a few simple yet powerful activities to re-engage with our incredibly creative mindset?

That's all it takes. And that's what this book is all about…a practical guide for developing your creative confidence. I call it your 'Creative Warrior'. Think of it as part muse, and part motivator. It's ready to help you achieve your goals and desires. It's there to help you make the changes to experience your life at its best. And what the Creative Warrior asks of you is simple…try a few fun and easy activities designed to help you break out of your comfort zone, gradually. No need to skydive. Yet.

I need to warn you now that connecting with your Creative Warrior is addictive. You will see ordinary things in ways you never have before. You will experience life as a non-stop journey of discovery.

Are you ready to ride the awesome power of creativity? I believe you are. Enjoy your flight!

Seth B. Greenwald
August 2018

Introduction

There is a definite natural progression to human activities. We learn to walk before we begin to run. We study our ABCs before we're ready to read. Addition comes before algebra. Mastering a fundamental skill is a prerequisite before moving up to the next level.

The same logic applies to mental activities. If our goal is to discover original ideas then first we must learn to be creative in our thinking. Creativity is about opening your mind to new possibilities. Thinking creatively is a powerful tool that you can use to generate new ideas and see the world in fresh ways. It can also improve areas of your life that, at first glance, you might not connect with creative thinking. For example, you may recapture that sense of wonder and awe you felt as a kid. You may discover deeper emotional connections with your friends and family. Creative thinking can, and will, open doors for you.

What is the best approach to take if we want to be more creative? Well, there are many techniques that I will show you. The key idea behind all of these is simple...keep an open mind. When you find yourself falling back into thoughts like "I have to do it this way" or "I don't know how to do it any other way"' then it's time to relax and practice with one of this book's mind-opening tips and techniques. These activities will help you rediscover a mindset ripe for creative endeavors.

This book consists of two sections. The "Pep Talks" chapters will describe what creativity is all about. These chapters are intended to put you in a proper mood before attempting the creativity-enhancing activities contained in the latter part of the book. These techniques are simple, easy-to-use exercises that can be practiced anytime to develop the creative powers you already possess. Yes, you already have fantastic creative potential. What you need is a push in the right direction to engage your power and put yourself on the path of the Creative Warrior.

When performing these exercises for the first time, give them your best effort. Take them seriously. However, if you find a particular technique is not working for you, move on to the next one. Don't worry if you're not making progress as quickly as you'd like. With a little patience and perseverance you'll see a change. It will happen, just don't give up.

I hope you have as much fun working with these activities as I had fun writing about them. I find that being able to think creatively is its own reward. Life becomes so much richer and more rewarding. Let my creative tools be the catalysts in reaching your goals. Try them out and experience what I'm talking about for yourself. And don't forget to have fun.

Part One: Pep Talks on Creativity

1 Explore Before You Bore

Life is all about making decisions.

Some are small: what do I want for dinner tonight? What should I wear to the prom? (Actually that last decision is a big one :)

Some are a bit bigger: Where should I go on summer vacation? What classes should I take this year?

And some are huge: What college do I want to go to? What should I major in? Who do I want to work for? What do I really want to do with my life?

Your decisions can lead you to where you want to go in life. It's the cumulative results of the choices you make on your life's journey that will help you reach the summit of your personal Mt. Everest. You'll need courage, confidence and perseverance to achieve your goals. However, there are many mountains in this wonderful world of ours. And they all seem worthwhile to climb. Which one do you choose? How do you select an option?

The problem is that our minds would prefer not to keep our options open for too long. No one likes feeling confused. We'd rather have a mountain to climb, sooner than later. That's all fine and good. What I'm proposing in this book is that you'll want to discover the many wonders of this world before you settle on a single path. You'll want to enjoy what you're doing and then try something different, just for the fun of it. You'll want to live your life like you did when you were a kid. With a sense of wonder and curiosity. You'll want to be comfortable with uncertainty because that's where the adventure lies.

It all boils down to experiencing multiple paths before you choose to commit to one. What I'm saying, in a nutshell, is 'explore before you bore'. Enjoy the journey. And here's the good news...your inner Creative Warrior is waiting to assist you whenever you are ready to explore!

2 The Way of the Creative Warrior

Life moves along quite effortlessly when we act out ingrained habits and routines. We do things because we're comfortable doing them. It feels good to live thinking we know what the future will bring.

Remember when you were a child and the world was new. Your mind was inquisitive and open to all experiences. Learning how the world worked was your main activity. You developed a mental picture of the world and through it became aware of where you fit in. We carry this conceptual world with us all through our lives. Without it we'd be lost.

Towards the end of our formative years the newness of the world rubs off and we convince ourselves that we know everything we need to know. Our inquisitive mind fades into the background and we ask fewer questions. Our learning process slows down. Soon after we may feel as if we're living life on auto-pilot.

Creative Warriors do things a bit differently. They keep a constant eye on their auto-pilot switch. They have an arsenal of tools to keep their eyes sharp and their minds supple. Creative Warriors use these tools to rattle their brains into inspired thought. These tools are the pep talks and techniques described in the following chapters.

Do you aspire to become a Creative Warrior? If the answer is yes, then keep reading. Try each activity and repeat the ones that work for you. Perform the techniques sincerely and you'll soon find yourself on the rewarding path of the Creative Warrior.

3 Just Have Fun

A Creative Warrior's first task is to bring ideas into the world. They aren't concerned with evaluating their value or relevancy. They're not interested in developing the best one. Nor do they wish to transform an idea into reality. The first step is simply to generate a multitude of ideas. We're after quantity, not quality. This book gives you the tools to succeed in ideation.

You may not agree with me now, but generating ideas is the fun part. No need to analyze or criticize. Why do you think children are so happy? It's because they're playing and having fun. They're using their imaginations to make up situations. They're taking new ideas out for a trial run. If the imaginary situation doesn't work for them, they drop it and find another one. Do they criticize themselves for choosing the wrong idea? Of course not. Young people are in it to have fun.

When you are in ideation mode remember the joy you felt as a kid. Remember how lighthearted you were when at play. It's really not hard to reconnect with the child inside of you. Remind yourself that it's your life and you want to have some fun.

4 Stomp on Your Fear

Have you ever heard someone say that they want to learn to draw but don't want to take a class because they don't know the first thing about drawing? Does that logic strike you as a bit strange? This applies to any skill...cooking, woodworking, writing, etc. Many people are afraid to try something new. There are numerous reasons for this unfortunate reaction and the common denominator is fear. Let's examine three fear-based obstacles and how you can overcome them.

Fear of not living up to your own expectations

Your self-image is a powerful motivator. But it may also hold you back from trying new things. Let's perform an exercise to determine if your self-image is holding you back or pushing you forward.

Close your eyes. Imagine yourself as an Olympic athlete. You pick the sport. Now imagine that you've just won the final competition and you're standing on the podium in third place. You receive your bronze medal. The crowd of 50,000 people burst into applause. So how do you feel right now? Are you proud of yourself and what you've accomplished? Or do you feel like a failure because you didn't win the competition?

If you felt like a failure, you self-image is going to cause you problems in the future. It's going to hold you back from trying something new because you can't imagine yourself not winning. Before you even start you'll be paralyzed by fear of failure. This is not good. What to do? Remind yourself that people are not born as successes. They work hard to get there. For example, think about Elvis Presley. Before he became the king of rock and roll, he was a truck driver. He was told by many record executives to stick with his day job as he'd never make it in the music industry. But he found ways to persevere through adversity and didn't let rejection affect how he saw himself...a success.

Fear of disappointing others

Day in and day out professional athletes play their game in front of tens of thousands of people. They don't hesitate to make their feelings known after a poor performance by their favorite players. That's part of the game of sports. But everyone has bad days; even multi-million dollar professionals. How do these athletes deal with their down days? They haven't gotten to their prominent positions by letting negative reactions throw them for a loop. They've discovered a way to not let it influence their play.

It's called being in the zone. By focused their attention on what they're doing, they can shut out the extraneous noise and distractions that would otherwise affect their game. Even if their play is a bit off, being in the zone will allow them to shrug off the negativity thrown their way. Hey, it's a tough world. Pro athletes must remain mentally strong through the rough times.

Fear of being the center of attention

A national poll was taken recently to determine what people were more afraid of: dying or public speaking. Believe it or not 90% of the respondents said public speaking. What is it about speaking in front of a group of people that strikes fear in our hearts? Many people are afraid of being exposed as a fraud. They fear that others will see that they really don't know what they're talking about.

There's an effective way to counteract that particular fear. You must prepare before taking the stage. Write an outline of what you will say. Don't just wing it. It doesn't need to be complicated. Just a few notes will help guide you through your presentation. Taking the time to prepare will convince yourself that you know what you're talking about. When in front of the group, focus on speaking slowly and clearly. It may feel awkward at first but you'll soon discover that speaking slower gives you confidence and asserts your presence. It also helps you to maintain your focus. Most activities worth doing are done in front of others. With enough preparation you'll enjoy being in the spotlight.

Don't let fear hold you back from the activities you want to participate in. Fear originates in your mind and causes your body to tense up. You can control fear because you create it. Therefore you have the power to destroy it. The first step is to become aware of the tension in your body. Then release it by focusing on it. The sooner you do this, the easier it will be to keep your fear in check. Stomp on your fear and become a Creative Warrior.

5 Your Seventh Sense

Many of us are well versed at analytical thinking. We've been taught to break a problem down into its constituent parts, define the relationships between the parts, and insert the parts into a pre-established formula and out pops the answer.

We've achieved much success with analysis. Our greatest technological achievements would not have transpired without the analytical/scientific methods we've established during the last 400 years. Science has convinced us to see the world mechanistically. The Earth revolves around the Sun in exactly 365.25 days. The Earth rotates fully on its axis in exactly 23 hours and 56 minutes. As you can see, and know, our lives are very time-oriented. But it wasn't always like that.

Believe it or not there once was a time before clocks. In fact, mechanical clocks are a relatively new invention. You may be wondering: without clocks how did we keep track of time? The answer is that we did it in a totally different way than we do today. If we need to know the time we simply look down at out wristwatch or cell phone. Numbers tell us all we need to know. When we want to get together with someone in the future we decide on a few more numbers.

Before clocks we still made plans, but we did it in a different way. Back then our time keeping was centered on the physical world. Instead of numbers, we used objects like the sun and moon. We were very much in touch with the world. Imagine a world without numbers or math. Our concepts of time and space would be totally different. For example, let's meet at 12:30 on Saturday at the park on Cedar Hill two miles north of town might convert to: let's meet at the highest point in town when the sun is a thumb's length to the right of the tallest oak tree in town.

It may seem a bit primitive to use your thumb to tell time because our highly analytical modern day minds are so used to working with abstraction that we've forgotten the advantages of working with our bodies. Or at least any part below our head.

If you want to become a Creative Warrior, you must reacquaint yourself with your body. You'll need to get in touch with the sensations and feelings that are flowing throughout every part of you. Our bodies are our connection to the world. We interact with the world through our seven senses. The first five are easy...eyes, ears, nose, tongue and skin. The sixth is our intellect which provides us an abstract representation of the world. It's what you imagine when you close your eyes and think about the world.

The seventh is a very important way of seeing which we often forget about but can't do without. We all have this seventh sense. Just like any of the other senses, the more you use it the stronger it becomes. Artists are the people with most developed sense of sight. Chefs have the strongest sense of taste. It follows that creative people have a more developed sense of intuition.

Intuition allows us to understand things without rational thought. We don't know how or why we know, but when an intuition pops into our heads we don't need to question the validity of it. It just is. An intuition can arrive at any time of the day. Your mind is working in the background without you even knowing it. Give it a problem to solve in the morning, take a break and an intuitive answer may pop into your mind in the evening or even while you are sleeping.

Creative Warriors know that to generate new ideas they must use all their senses especially intuition. Analytical thinking will only take you so far. You need to trust your holistic thinking abilities (intuition) when on the path of the Creative Warrior.

6 Creative Warriors are Fearless

Connecting with our creativity is scary at first. It involves taking an honest look at one's true self. We need to see ourselves as we are, not as we want to be. For many people this is too much to bear. It means seeing our failures as well as our successes. Seeing our ugliness in addition to our beauty. It means acknowledging that we may not be the rock stars we thought we were. Like I said, scary stuff.

The upside to all this honesty is a complete understanding of who we are right now. It's an eye-opening process. And it can hurt. The self-image we've taken so long to build up may collapse in an instant. Honesty cuts deep. If you hope to reach your creative self, you must expect to hurt a little bit.

This experience is not something to fear, but something to embrace. The truth is that a shallow person will produce shallow work. A person who explores the depth of his psyche may produce something meaningful. You can only understand the outer world by going inside yourself. If this sounds like a paradox then you get it. The better you know yourself, the more clearly you'll perceive the world. It's the yin-yang principle come to life in you.

Creative Warriors are fearless. They are willing to explore the unchartered depths of their souls. The unknown realms of their psyches are their playground. They return to this place again and again for they know that true creativity will only be discovered from within.

7 Kitchen Creativity

Reality cooking shows are fun to watch. A very popular one promises the aspiring chefs $10,000 if they win the competition. The rules are simple: given a basket of random ingredients, make a dish that tastes and looks better than the other contestants' entries. The three judges watch the contestants prepare their creations, but are not allowed to give feedback until the end of the competition when they are presented with the dish each chef has whipped up.

The ingredients in each contestant's basket are identical. And the parameters for creation are simple: make an appetizer or an entree or a dessert. On the particular episode I watched they were asked to make a dessert from the following ingredients: celery, tortilla chips, mint and strawberry popsicles. Each ingredient taken alone suggested a different type of dessert. Though, frankly I have never associated celery with dessert.

Getting to the final round of the show is not easy. The two very talented competitors immediately found a way to combine the ingredients. The contestants were given twenty minutes to complete their dishes. No additional time was given to add finishing touches. Lots of pressure left little time to think. But these aspiring chefs knew what they wanted to create and went about doing it.

Chef A, let's call him Alex, set off to the refrigerator to retrieve milk and cream. His idea was combine all the ingredients, except the celery, into a very smooth ice cream. The celery was mixed with wine to make a side dish to cleanse the palate. Alex caramelized the tortilla chips and served them as a very crunchy topping.

Chef B, Belinda, decided to combine all the ingredients including the celery. She found a loaf of bread and eggs and mixed all the ingredients in a bowl. Belinda was off to make a bread pudding. A few minutes later the concoction was dished into ramekins and baked into the oven. You could tell that the judges' mouths were watering.

Ice cream versus bread pudding. Cool and warm. Liquid and solid. Creamy with a crunchy topping and chewy with a soft inside. Could any two desserts be more different? Amazingly they both were made from very similar ingredients.

Lesson learned: there are no limitations when it comes to creativity. The exact same problem stated in the exact same way can be resolved with completely different solutions. And I bet that if there were a couple more contestants, they would also have come up with creative dessert ideas.

Both of the desserts were praised by the judges. There wasn't a strong preference between the two. In other words, there was no right or wrong solution to the problem. Both desserts achieved a similar level of success by combining the ingredients in a very tasty and visually appealing way. This popular television show proves that with a creative mindset you can generate multiple ideas that are all different while solving the same problem.

8 Try a New Mustard

I was in the supermarket the other day. Since it was mid-summer, I went to the condiment aisle to replenish my supply of accessories for my favorite grilled food...hot dogs. What I saw there amazed me. I knew there were many varieties of mustards, but never actually conducted a survey. I counted 46 distinct varieties of this very popular condiment. They came in all manner of size, shapes, colors and flavors. Classic yellow was there right next to whiskey-infused. Dijon sat close to a honey hybrid. There were even fruit flavored mustards. When did this happen?!

When I was a kid there were just two types of mustards...yellow and off yellow. Then came Dijon. These three varieties were all you had to choose from. Now our choices have multiplied by a factor of 16. Are there too many choices to deal with?

Typically we tend to stop searching when we find a mustard we like. This one becomes our favorite. We put it on a pedestal. We may even dig our heels in and defend our favorite when we see other people enjoying different variety of mustard. Becoming defensive over mustard? Hmmm, curious.

We act this way over things other than mustard. Clothes, shoes and hair styles. Sports teams, religion and politics. These are just a few examples. It appears we can become defensive over almost anything. Whenever there's more than one option, we simply choose a side and then build a case as to why our selection is the best. We become deaf and blind to the good things the other options offer. We build up the superiority of our own selection and find fault with all others. What's the best mustard to put on a hot dog? Well, we really can't answer this question honestly without trying all 46 varieties first. Maybe we've tried three, four or even six different types. Forty more to go.

The same argument goes for ideas. When we find one we like, we stop searching. We close the door to alternatives. However it's the alternatives that allow us to see beyond what we already know. A Creative Warrior knows that taking alternative ideas out for a trial run can open us up to the spicy variety of life.

9 A Journey of Discovery

We are very busy people. The hours in our busy day are limited so we need to be efficient with our time. That explains why we are constantly on the go. To complete our To Do lists quickly we need to know where we are headed at all times. Or do we?

The activities we choose to accomplish pull us forward in time. We visualize our intended end result and then imagine a way to get there. We feel in control. But is there an alternate way to work?

For example, as I'm writing this chapter I don't know where I'll ultimately wind up. More specifically, I have a general idea of the direction in which I'm heading, but I don't have a clear destination in mind. I see the path under my feet with each step I take. However, there is no path at all a few steps ahead. This way of working puts me in a constant state of discovery.

Most people are not accustomed to this frame of mind. Most people are pulled forward by the picture of the destination or goal they imagine. For those people it's all about figuring out what is the best way to reach their goals. In other words, they know where they want to go but not how to get there.

On the opposite end of the spectrum are people who don't have a fixed destination in mind when they begin their journey. Notice I said "fixed destination." For these people the end result is not set in stone because they allow it to change as they move forward. They are on a constant journey of discovery knowing not what they'll find around the next bend.

As I mentioned earlier, I am writing this chapter with no fixed destination in mind. It's exciting to work like this. It allows me to enter into a state where time slows down and I can gain a hyper-awareness of my present situation. I see and hear more clearly. I feel a deeper connection with the people and things around me. I don't feel pulled by the future because I am anchored in the now moment. In other words, I am enjoying the journey.

It's not hard to experience this powerful state of mind for yourself. I do it by writing. You can do it with any activity you choose. All you need to do is remember these three simple guidelines:

1. Don't worry about where you're going.

2. Stay focused in the present moment. Don't look back, don't look forward.

3. Experience the journey as if you're traveling it for the first time.

Now be on your way. Take your first step. Keep an open mind and enjoy being on the creative path.

10 You Can't Beat that New Car Experience

Every three years my grandfather would religiously drive his beautifully maintained Cadillac Coupe de Ville down to the dealership where he had bought it three years earlier. The salesman would show him each and every new car on the lot. Sometimes the salesman would take my grandfather for a ride around the neighborhood in a gleaming new convertible. Other times he'd let my grandfather drive down the highway in a powerful new coupe.

After the ride the salesman would ask how he felt about the new car. My grandfather would reply politely that he enjoyed the ride but he wanted to stick with the most updated version of his beloved Cadillac Coupe de Ville. It wasn't an exact match that my grandfather wanted. He'd be sure to ask for a different color or detailing. Or switch over from leather to a suede interior. One year he went radical and moved from a two door coupe to a four door sedan. The changes really didn't matter. As long as he was driving off the lot in a new car he was happy.

Why was my granddad satisfied with a slightly newer version of the same car he had driven in? It wasn't about money; as the cost of new car was always more than the trade-in price. Did he feel safer? Not really. Better gas mileage? No. Comfort? Nah. Was it status? Doubtful as the neighbors never noticed. So what compelled him to buy a new car every three years?

I'm convinced he had a more basic psychological reason. It's such a basic need that we typically don't notice the influence it has on our decision-making process. It's similar to the feeling I get upon waking each morning. Don't you feel a palpable excitement for what lies ahead? It's the start of the day that gets me energized. Everything seems new again.

And I believe that is the reason my grandfather would spent money on a car he really didn't need. He was after the feeling of *NEW*. New car smell. New car sound. New car look. But it goes even deeper than that. He wasn't excited about getting a new car. That was simply the vehicle (no pun intended) for his new experiences. In other words, he was turned on by how the new car made him feel. A new smell, new sound, new sight...these are the things my grandfather loved. The only reason he waited for three years to trade in his car was because that's when the lease expired. Had there would have been an opportunity to buy a new car every year I'm sure he would have gone for it. The feeling of new is that powerful.

Are you interested in becoming more creative? New experiences and sensations will get you there. They will help you break out of the habitual ways you've always done things. You'll see the world with fresh eyes. Think about the world in original ways. Try it for yourself. Keep an open mind. Maintain a strong spirit. A new world awaits you. In that new world you'll learn how to become a Creative Warrior.

11 Kickers Don't Make Good Quarterbacks

When I think, I typically think in words. For example, my to do lists are typically written in full sentences. Sometimes I'll draw out what I need to do in pictures. But this approach is less common. Approximately 75% of all people use words to make sense of the world. In psychological parlance, these people are called left-brainers because that's where linguistic center of the brain is located. The other hemisphere of the brain, the right side, sees the world in images and symbols.

We have these two hemispheres because we need both to function. When we want to drill down and analyze something, we engage our left brain. If we need to step back and see relationships among things, we utilize our right brains. Different strokes for different tasks. That's all it is. One is not better than the other. Is a fork better than a spoon? No, they're just used for different jobs.

A Creative Warrior wants to generate multiple ideas. This is not what our left brains are good at. Logic will get you from point A to point B. Start with a problem, follow the proven process and you'll find yourself with the answer. Notice I said "the" answer. Logic is a linear approach that allows only one answer. Math problems make good use of logic to arrive at a solution. That's because there are unchanging absolutes in the mathematical world. 2+2=4. A circle always has 360 degrees. Two parallel lines will never cross. If you divide a number by itself, you'll always get one. See what I mean. Follow the rules and you'll find the answer.

The right brain is a different story. This is where imagination rules the roost. Give your brain a problem and it'll come up with as many alternatives as time permits. Notice I said alternatives as opposed to answers. Right brainers know that to be creative one must not begin the evaluation process until all the ideation phase is over. Leave the assessment for the left brains because that's what left brains do.

Do you watch football? If so, you know that certain types of players make certain type of plays. For example, a coach would not ask a field goal kicker to take a handoff from the quarterback and run the ball. He has running backs that do that. In baseball, there are pitchers and there are catchers. Each position comes with a specialized skill. So too do the two hemispheres of the brain.

The problem arises when we try to evaluate when we are in ideation mode, or conversely, attempt to generate ideas when we are in the midst of analyzing them. The brain works well when it has some momentum. It doesn't like starting and stopping. Similarly car engines don't respond well to that type of action either. Now ask yourself: if you wouldn't want to treat your car poorly, why would you want to hurt your brain?

Don't take it too hard. Unlike cars, our brain didn't come with an owner's manual. Do you really need to know what goes on inside your head? No, because you learn by doing. You become aware of which actions work to get you closer to your goal and which actions move you farther from where you want to be.

Remember to match your brain to the situation. Use your right hemisphere for brainstorming purposes and your left one for evaluation. Doing this will put you on the path of the Creative Warrior.

12 Lessons Learned from Creative Geniuses

Creative geniuses don't come along very often. But when they do, inspiring ideas and inventions follow. Geniuses do not have patents on the creative process. All of us have the potential for great creativity. So the question becomes….what can we learn from these individuals that will improve our own creativity?

In creative fields such as art, architecture and design, the work process is rarely linear. In other words, the road from initial idea to finished expression will not be a straight one. Inspiration can come from any direction, at any time and completely change the character and course of the original idea. However, instead of getting upset or disoriented by this intrusion, open-minded individuals will incorporate this new energy into their thinking process and move on. In fact, they will deliberately find a way to invite inspiration into their creative process because they know that the end result will often be an innovative resolution.

The AHA! moment is associated with creative geniuses. Archimedes is sitting in his bathtub and EUREKA! he realizes the concept of buoyancy. The Buddha is sitting under a bodhi tree and POOF! he understands the nature of reality. How about Einstein's thought experiments? Sitting at his breakfast table imagining what it would be like to ride on a beam of light and BANG! the theory of relativity is born. Edison took a twenty minute nap at his work table and CLICK! the world would never be dark again.

Are you thinking that this only happens to geniuses and it'll never happen to you? Well if that's the case why did Edison describe creative genius as 1% inspiration and 99% perspiration? Sure the 1% AHA moment gets all the publicity. But I'm convinced it could happen to anyone if we put the remaining 99% of our time to good use.

Let's assume that we know our subject matter very well. (That's the perspiration part). Is there a technique we can use to usher in an inspirational moment? Lucky for us there are many ways. So let's see what we can learn from the top three creative geniuses of all time......Leonardo da Vinci, Thomas Edison and Albert Einstein.

Leonardo da Vinci

This amazing individual, born in Italy in 1452, is widely considered the most creative person of all time. His numerous artistic contributions were spread throughout the fields of painting, architecture and engineering. *The Mona Lisa*, da Vinci's masterpiece is arguably the most famous painting in history. The woman portrayed in the painting was the wife of a client of da Vinci's named Lisa del Giocondo. The enigmatic expression she wears is both alluring and aloof at the same time. The technique which da Vinci used to create this ambiguous smile is called sfumato, which in Italian means "without lines or borders" or "evaporate like smoke". Look closely at the corners of the Mona Lisa's mouth and you'll see that it's very hard to tell if the shadows are a result of the smile or whether the smile is the result of the shadows. That's a perfect example of the concept of sfumato applied to painting.

You may be asking yourself: what does all this have to do with my creativity? Well, let's take the concept of sfumato and apply it to our lives. Have you ever approached a new situation in the same way as you've always done simply because you felt you had no time or energy to explore new possibilities? Everyone has. We don't question our first reaction to situations. We accept our initial interpretation as hard fact.

Now ask yourself what would happen if you realized that your first reaction is just one of many possible responses to a particular situation? You would be free to choose the most appropriate response. Instead of seeing things in terms of right/wrong, good/bad or black/white, you would realize that there is actually a continuum of possible resolutions to the same problem. And this continuum lies between the dualistic endpoints of the black/white spectrum. This is the gray area. But watch out. Many people find exploring this area to be an uncomfortable experience. It feels messy and uncertain. The solid ground has now turned into a muddy field. But do not despair because this is where the real opportunity for creativity lies. The more you are comfortable with this messy gray area, the more creative you will become.

So next time you're feeling constrained by the "way things have always been done", remember to get comfortable with the gray, accept the uncertainty and embrace the ambiguity. Take a break and consider *Mona Lisa's* enigmatic smile. Your AHA moment could be a moment away.

Thomas Edison

Did you know that this brilliant man, born in 1847 in Ohio, holds the world's record for patents with 1,093? He received his first patent at the age of 21. That's more than 17 patents for the next 63 years of his life! With so many patents to his name his idea generation process must have been incredible. In fact, he imposed an "idea quota" on himself. He demanded a minor invention every ten days and a major invention every six months. That's a lot of pressure to put on oneself, but Edison found a way to thrive.

At first glance extreme goal setting may seem to inhibit rather than encourage creativity. It may seem too restrictive a process to support ideation. And this argument may be true if used inappropriately. But Edison did not limit the type of ideas he was interested in. Nor did he limit his thoughts. He simply gave himself a quantifiable target to aim for. Edison realized that the mind seeks to accomplish what is expected of it. And it helps if the goal is specific. Edison understood that his conscious, rational intellect was only one aspect of his mind.

The mind never rests. Even when the body is asleep the subconscious mind continues to work. For example, did you ever forget someone's name and no matter how hard you tried you couldn't remember it? Then you went to sleep and the next thing you know you woke up clearly remembering the name. That's because your mind was working during the night without any conscious effort on your part.

Edison recognized the power of the subconscious mind and perfected a technique to promote creativity. We call it the power nap. Edison would climb up on his work table and sleep for twenty minutes. He wasn't in a deep sleep, nor was he fully awake. But he noticed that while in this in-between state, called the hypnogogic, great insights on the particular problems he was trying to resolve while awake would occur. Edison trained himself to stay in this state of mind for as long as he could and as a result his level of creativity increased dramatically.

Now I'm not suggesting that you hop onto your desk and take a snooze. That just wouldn't be prudent. What I'm suggesting is that give yourself a break every now and then. If you feel stuck, take a walk. If you feel trapped let your mind wander. Will this technique work for you? Try it and find out.

Albert Einstein

This man, widely considered the most brilliant human being in history, was born in Germany in 1879. The publication of his 1905 scientific paper Special Theory of Relativity would forever change the way we understand the world. So if we were to ask this man how he was able to be so creative, what would he say? Would it have something to do with going to school? Or working long hours in the lab? Maybe eat right and exercise? None of the above. What he did say on this subject is simply this: The secret to creativity is knowing how to hide your sources.

Hmmm...at first glance it appears as if Einstein is condoning plagiarism. Could this be? To find an answer let's look at what this great man accomplished during his lifetime. Einstein's devoted his life to unifying the Newtonian laws of mechanics with the laws of the electromagnetic field. He never quite got there but his work fundamentally changed the way we view the world. Einstein utilized mathematics to develop his ideas and prove the validity of his theories. He did not perform any experiments as Edison did nor did he bring about any useful inventions as da Vinci did. In fact after graduating from the Zurich School of Technology, Einstein could not find a job in the field of physics. He worked at the Swiss Patent office as an evaluator of applications for electromagnetic devices. Einstein understood the value of using other physicist's ideas as the starting point for his own work.

You may ask….is this ethical? Of course. Einstein was not interested in simply copying other people's work. What he did was to build on the borrowed idea until it was unrecognizable and subsumed by his own original thinking. In his own words, he knew how to hide his sources.

This is the way we all must work. I'm sure you've heard the expression: there is nothing new under the sun. It's so true. We would be wise to accept the fact that the most efficient way to new ideas and creativity is to understand and acknowledge the good work that others already have done. But don't stop there. Add to that work. Develop it. Forge ahead on your own path. That is the way of Creative Warrior.

We all have the potential for exceptional creativity. It's just that most of us were taught from an early age that the "artsy" stuff is for the few people who were born with a gift. But it's not art that is needed. It's our acceptance of uncertainty, it's the power of our subconscious mind and it's building on other people's ideas that will show us the way to inspired thoughts.

13 Brainstorm Before Evaluation

Problems, problems, problems. We are constantly bombarded with issues that need our attention. A problem exists anytime there is a gap between what you currently have and what you want to achieve in the future. Problems can run the gamut from routine ones like what to make for dinner to complex social issues like acting responsibly to help to reduce pollution.

The first step in the problem-solving process is to identify the issue you are working on. There are two main approaches. We can either first define the problem and then work towards a solution. Or we can turn that logic on its head and identify what we want to achieve (end state) and then work backwards to define the steps we'll need to get there. Whichever method you choose, you'll want to use Creative Warrior techniques to get there.

Why do we need to be creative when solving problems? Because the first solution that comes to mind is rarely the best one. We must generate a few alternatives so we can evaluate the strengths and weaknesses of each in order to choose the one with the highest value for us. First we brainstorm then we evaluate. Be careful not to mix the two as they are two very distinct mindsets.

Brainstorming is about coming up with alternatives. Evaluation is about making choices. I'm not suggesting anything negative about evaluation. My point is that in order to make a decision between all the ideas that were generated by brainstorming, we must stop ideation and begin assessing the stockpile of ideas we have in front of us.

Remember that brainstorming and evaluation are two very different mental processes. It's not so easy to switch between these two modes quickly. It's best to begin evaluation only after you are completely finished with brainstorming.

14 Where Creativity Lives

The world is a frenetic place. Tune in any time to experience a cacophony of sights and sounds around you. We're accustomed to looking out into this phenomenal world. There's much to learn by interacting with the world around us.

Turn your gaze inward and you'll find an equally active world. Your thoughts, sensations and emotions form a world of their own. Complex and rich, it's a world you'll want to be comfortable with in order to find your creativity.

Words are fun to dissect. Look at the word insight. Break it into two parts: in-sight. Seeing in to yourself. Can a word be any more self-explanatory? If we want to gain insight and discover ideas then we must begin to explore our inner world.

Similar to the phenomenal world, your inner world is a place pulsing with activity. Full color memories of long ago mingle with freshly minted experiences of yesterday. Sights, sounds and images are waiting there for you take hold of them.

Creative Warriors know that it's not enough to use your eyes to see. We must look inward for an intuitive grasp of reality. That's where we'll find our creativity.

15 Steer Clear from Fear

I want you to think about the times in your life
when you were optimistic and hopeful. Your mood
was upbeat and positive. It felt like nothing could
bring you down. Your mind was open and clear.

Now turn away from that mind state and experience
being afraid. Your mood turns eerily dark. Your
confidence is low. You can't think straight or sit still.

Creativity depends on being open to the world
around you and engaged with the one inside you. A
mind wrapped in fear is numb and insensitive. The
last thing it wants to do is consider new ideas.

To encourage creativity you must steer clear of fear
and summon up your courageous self. Find a quiet
and calming place. Don't worry about the events of
the past. Don't be afraid of what the future holds.
Focus on the thoughts that enter your mind. Look
at each with a gentle gaze. Don't try to analyze or
hold on to them. Enjoy this time…it's just you and
your creative flow.

16 Be You

Each of us sees the world in our own unique way. We each have a unique perspective shaped by our environment, our experiences and our upbringing.

Do you ever feel that there is no difference between you and people close to you? Your thinking goes something like this: I'm the same height, weight and age as they are. I went to the same school and do the same job as they do. Even my house looks the same as theirs.

Well, that's your brain being lazy. It's finding similarities only. Ask it to work a little harder and find your uniqueness. For example, I'm 5'-9", he's 5'-11". I weigh 115, she weighs 125. I have brown eyes, hers are hazel.

Your mind is a powerful tool. It can make you think you are just one in the crowd. Or it can identify what is special about you. Which way will you go? Hint: Creative Warriors embrace what is unique and different about themselves.

17 A Creative Warrior's Courageous Dream

The Creative Warrior has not always been fearless. He has let the criticism of others eat at his soul. He has allowed ridicule to weigh heavy on his thoughts. He was once a sieve for the entire world's pettiness. Lacking confidence and conviction, he did not possess the strength needed to support creative expressiveness.

Alone in his room, he would attempt to connect with the source of his creative power. Book in hand, he would dutifully follow the instructions. Over and over he would read what he must do. He waited patiently for an idea, any idea. Nothing. Insecurity arrived with a disturbing thought: what if I'm just not good enough to become a Creative Warrior?

Like a boxer hit by a low punch, he felt the air leave his lungs. Snippets of his life flashed before his eyes. He was near his breaking point when the inspiring thought suddenly arrived: what would happen if I just didn't care about what others thought about me? And then another: I don't need approval from anyone to think the way I think; my thoughts work for me.

This was a revelation. He had never let thoughts like these see the light of day. He had thwarted them by denying their relevance. Today was different. He rationalized it as an experiment. If nothing good came of these blasphemous ideas, he would never again drop his guard.

Just then something flittered across his consciousness. A tiny germ of an idea that he couldn't quite grasp, though he understood its tone. It filled him with a feeling of hope. He decided that he'd wait until it came back. Five minutes, ten minutes. Nothing. An hour later he knew it was time to take a break and get some food.

After dinner he decided to take a nap. Out quickly but not deeply he began to daydream. Thoughts of the day's events passed by like wispy clouds on a summer afternoon. Suddenly the clouds gathered overhead and a lightning bolt hit: "I do have what it takes to be a Creative Warrior. All I need to do is believe in myself and persevere with courage." With that thought, he knew he had found the path of the Creative Warrior.

18 Remember Your Strengths

You'll find a good deal of wisdom packaged in quotes. Consider this one: the grass is always greener on the other side. We accept it as true, but what does it really mean?

The quote implies that we are quick to compare ourselves to other people and envious of what we see. The bottom line is we want what they have. This mentality of inferiority puts us in a position of weakness because it forces us to spend much of our lives focused on how to acquire what we don't already have. The sad fact is that it's a never ending cycle. We are never satisfied with what we have.

To break this vicious circle we need to put ourselves in a position of strength. We need to realize that what we already possess is what makes us who we are. We must apply this perspective to not only our material wealth, but our skills and abilities as well.

Does this mean we should not strive to learn more and be more? No. It means that we must stand tall and be proud! We are unique individuals with our own way of doing things. A Creative Warrior knows that remembering our strengths will provide us with the courage and confidence to navigate competently when faced with unfamiliar situations.

19 Ideas are like Salmon

Imagine an iceberg. The section poking above the water represents your conscious mind: rational, analytical and comfortable with facts. What lies under the water is unknown to you, but it exists, as does your subconscious mind. You don't see what it's working on, but eventually you will see the results.

Your job is to listen to your subconscious mind. Its job is to make sense of the world around you. When your subconscious is ready, it will send a packet of information up to your consciousness. Some people call it an idea. Others call it intuition. Still others refer to it as inspiration. Whatever you call it, it's still the same thing. Your job is to take this packet of information seriously. You need to be alert because it may come bubbling up to the surface at any time. Be ready to write it down, sketch it up or record it in any way you prefer. These flashes of inspiration can be very fleeting. Like a dream upon waking, if you don't capture it, it'll be gone in a flash.

Creative Warriors are experts at not interfering in the work of their subconscious minds. They are always ready to catch an idea that has just popped out of the murky depths. Think of yourself as a big brown bear waiting on high alert for a salmon to jump out of a beautiful Alaskan stream. I'm there, are you?

20 Stay Loose, Move On

It's natural to begin a project with the end state in mind. We identify a particular outcome which we expect to reach within a defined timeframe. We develop a plan of action. We focus on completing each step of the plan with the expectation of achieving our goal.

This is the way we've always done it. Our plan defines our path. That's fine but we must remember to ask ourselves if there are other ways. Creative Warriors know that there always are. These alternative approaches won't necessarily be better than the one we're working with. Or maybe they will. Let's be flexible and keep our minds supple and eyes open for new ideas.

I'm not suggesting that we immediately change our direction. Instead let's explore these newly hatched possibilities without trashing our current one. Try to use the new ideas to complement or transform what we are already doing. Stay loose and enjoy the journey as we travel towards our destination.

21 The Ever-Expanding Box

It feels good to question the way things are. As we search for answers, we define a world for ourselves. Each of us is busy creating our own reality. The phenomenal world is enormous and may make us feel small. The truth is that we understand the world via a limited perspective.

Many people feel uncomfortable when their worldview is questioned. These individuals think their way is the only way. They feel grounded, safe and in control of their lives. There is nothing wrong with wanting to feel comfortable.

The problem arises when we think we know everything and stop asking questions. At that point we cut ourselves off from new experiences. We create a box and lock ourselves inside. No new ideas come in, no new ideas go out.

It's all a delusion. We can never create a box big enough to contain our whole world. I'm not saying it's wrong to create the box. I'm saying that we must remember to allow the box to expand beyond the limits of what we already know. There are always new things to see, new places to visit, new people to meet.

By opening ourselves up to new experiences, we remind ourselves that the way we understand the world is merely one of 7 billion ways... and counting. Creative Warriors know that their own way is not the only way.

The flip side is that when we see ourselves as just one of many, we can feel small and unimportant. That's when our ego awakens. It tells us that we are important and special. It may even want us to close the box again. That's the little voice we must learn to ignore. We must remain inquisitive. Remain open to the wonders of the world and find your creative path.

22 Listen to Your Gut

Some people refer to their "gut" when talking about their subconscious mind. Beware! Your rational head may disagree with your gut. To protect its dominance when the gut tosses up a new idea, your head may launch a thought like: that's not the right way to do things or you've never done it like that before. Your head is trying to convince you to stop thinking in new ways.

Your head wants to analyze which idea is the best one. That's what your head is good at. But it's your job to convince your head to stay out of your gut's way until the ideation process is over. There will be plenty of time to evaluate ideas later. Your gut is your creative engine. Learn to let it do its job without interference and you'll be on the Creative Warrior's path.

23 Letter to the Author

Dear Author,

I am intrigued by your book title "Secrets of a Creative Warrior" and would like to know more about it. I don't consider myself very creative and prefer to stay that way. I do things the way I do because that's the way I've always done them. I do the same things each day because I know what to expect. I'm not fond of surprises and I like to feel comfortable. So why should I try to do things differently? I just don't see how that type of behavior would benefit me, though I'm willing to hear you out.

Sincerely,
Okay with my life as is

Dear Okay,

I understand where you are coming from. I was once there too. Let me tell you the story of how creativity changed my life. Many years ago I began to see people wearing a tee shirt that said "Choose Life". For the longest time I didn't understand what that meant. We are alive, what choice do we really have? Maybe the designer of this shirt was sending a message about suicide. Or maybe he was against abortion. Either way it wasn't a tee shirt I wanted to wear.

A few years later I began to see people wearing another tee shirt with a similar message. This one stated "Life is Good." Something about that shirt resonated with me. It made me think about my life. Was my life good? This was a fundamental question which I needed to answer.

On a blank sheet of paper I made two columns. The one on the left I labeled: things that are good about my life. The right column was entitled: things that are bad about my life. I filled in the columns by examining every aspect of my life. When I was done I was surprised to find that the two columns were similar in length. No definite answer. I was disappointed and about to quit when an inspiring thought came to me. Most of the things in my life belong in a third column labeled: things that are just okay about my life. Well then, how was I going ever going to wear the *Life is Good* shirt? Maybe I should design a *Life is Just Okay* shirt. That's a bit depressing I said to myself. Is that how I really feel? Why am I so passive about the things I do in my life? Then the cathartic moment came when the image of the *Choose Life* shirt popped into my head.

I realized that the real meaning of choosing life is more than a sentiment about anti-abortion or anti-suicide. It's deeper than that. Our lives are made up of one present moment moving in to the next one. There really is no other way to live and experience things except in the moment. Yet we ignore the present in favor of looking at what's past or thinking about what lies ahead. Our heads are filled with thoughts such as: as soon as I get a better job, I'll be able to stop searching and enjoy my life. Or if I can just meet the person of my dreams my real life will begin. Sadly many people never achieve the ideal conditions they've imagined for themselves. And they never find a way to choose their own life as is and enjoy the experiences that come their way each day.

Dear Okay, you may be wondering what all this talk about living in the moment has to offer has to do with creativity. My book will introduce you to activities to help you become a Creative Warrior. These techniques are all about showing you ways to maintain your awareness of the present moment. They will show you how to open up and appreciate whatever is happening in your life right now. They will show you how to approach life so that you may experience things in new ways. And finally, they will help you to break free of your habitual way of perceiving the world. By taking the path of the Creative Warrior you'll learn to see with fresh eyes and think with a clear mind to reach your ultimate goal...to discover new ideas. I encourage you to turn the page and read on. Your creative journey begins now...

Enjoy,
The Author

Part Two: Techniques to Inspire Creativity

24 Just Scribble

You don't need to be an artist to be creative. It doesn't even require for you to consider yourself artistic. In fact, that idea will just get in the way of reaching your creative potential.

Find a pencil and paper and start to scribble. Notice I didn't say begin to draw. Why? Drawing implies that you have an idea or image in mind which you want to capture on paper. I'm simply asking you to move your pencil without stopping to evaluate your work. Remember that you're not trying to draw any thing in particular.

Continue scribbling for at least five minutes. Don't listen when your inner critic says that your scribbles look like a child could have made them. That's the point. Children are naturally creative and express themselves without much self-editing. That's the feeling you want to recapture. Just stay loose and go where your creative impulses take you.

You don't need to produce a work of art. Your scribbles may transform itself into some thing that you recognize and want to develop. That's fine, go for it. Alternatively, your scribbles may remain an abstract pattern that makes sense to only you. Wonderful. What if your scribbles simply remain scribbles? No problem.

When you were a kid you didn't concern yourself with heady ideas. Your goal was to play and have fun. Go back to those carefree times. Feel the playfulness you once felt. The point of this exercise is to get your creative juices moving. Let the work take you where it will. Don't fight the free flowing, not-in-control feeling. Be bold and embrace that feeling. A Creative Warrior knows that there's much to learn from one's inner child.

25 Fred Flintstone Eats Cactus While Driving

Ideas don't always show up when we want them to. They may not even come at all. Yet there are certain techniques that you can use to coax ideas out from their hiding spots. In times of idea drought you need to remind yourself that ideas are there. In fact, there's a large idea reservoir waiting for you to find it. Think oil. It could take weeks or even months of drilling to find the untapped pool of black gold hidden deep below the surface. An oil man may come up dry his first few attempts. But once he finds it, EUREKA! he's got it for good.

It's the same situation when drilling for ideas. The good news is that it won't take much money, equipment or time to find them. There's much hard rock between the drill and the oil reservoir. Similarly, there's mind-stuff between your conscious mind and your ideas. But don't give up. Each time you drill for ideas you'll get closer to the source. Then one day you'll connect and will know the way for good.

The first step when drilling for ideas is to relax. Creativity and anxiety don't work well together. Find a comfortable chair in a quiet place. Let whatever issues you are worrying about float away. Close your eyes and try focus on the sounds around you. The focus I'm talking about is more of a loose grasp than a tight fist. Listen to the sounds you hear now. You've heard the expression "go with the flow." That's what I want you to do. Don't think, just listen. Hear the highs and the lows. The rough shrills and the smooth hums. Don't think "oh, that's just an old car rumbling." Try not to think in words at all. Stay focused on the sounds. If a thought comes into your mind let it flow out of your consciousness so that you may come back to the present moment. No need to castigate yourself for letting thoughts in. Just come back. This is about experiencing the reality of sound in real time. So often we forget to tune into what's going on around us. Instead we're planning for the future and worrying about the past. We need to give ourselves opportunities to tune into the present moment. It's a very uplifting feeling. Very different from the heavy analytical mindset we are so used to. Experience it once and you will be hooked.

Now that you are relaxed and focused in the moment, it's time to come up with ideas. I'm not talking about just one. I'm suggesting that you come up with at least ten ideas. I know it sounds difficult now, but trust me, and more importantly, trust yourself that you will be able to come up with ten ideas in ten minutes or less. And here's how you'll do it.

First place a blank piece of paper and pen in front of you. Now think about an object. Any object will do. For this exercise, choose a car. Choose a type of car that you've enjoyed riding in or hope to ride in one day. Red Maserati coupe. Yellow Lamborghini convertible. Hey don't hold back, it's your time now. Imagine your car speeding down a highway. No one else is on the road. Visualize the landscape whizzing by. Trees, water, desert, whatever comes to mind.

Imagine that you are a passenger in the car. There is no driver. You can make the car go wherever you want just by thinking about it. But this car is not an ordinary car. It can also fly in the air, glide on water and tunnel underground. Sort of a luxurious chitty chitty bang bang vehicle. With all this potential at your disposal, what do you do next? Do you stay on the road? Fly towards the moon? Cut right through a mountain? It's your choice.

Now look around the car and imagine that you are riding with anyone in the world you want to be with. They could be alive, deceased or an imaginary character. There is no limit to who is in the car with you. Fred Flintstone, Marilyn Monroe, George Washington, your future boyfriend or your great-great grandmother. It's a dream come true, so take advantage of it.

Your job now is to observe. Listen to the conversations that your fellow passengers are having. Do you hear them speaking about their relationships? Food? Future plans? If they are attempting to start a conversation with you then by all means interact with them. Let your responses flow naturally from your subconscious mind. You want to stay in your semi-dream state for as long as possible.

When you are ready to come back to your normal conscious state do it slowly. It's similar to waking from a dream. You don't want to jar yourself awake because you'll need to hang on to as many memories of your wild car trip as possible. As soon as you are ready, pick up the pen in front of you and write down everything you can remember. Places, characters, relationships, conversations, odd objects you saw along the way. Just write. No need to edit now. You want a large stockpile of ideas to choose from later when you begin to focus on which one to develop further. Remember that one of the keys to brainstorming is not to evaluate your ideas as you are generating them. That's a surefire way to kill your creative flow. Just let the ideas come. Don't accept or reject them. No idea is stupid. It's all about quantity at this point.

Look at the list of words that your imaginary car ride has helped you to come up with. Pick three at random. Now put them together in a sentence. It doesn't need to make sense. This is just another way to stimulate your creative flow. Here's an off-the-wall sentence from my wild ride: Fred Flintstone eats cactus while driving. Here's another one: Marilyn Monroe got married to my grandfather during a tennis match. Try it for yourself. The ideas need not be sensible. Don't force them to conform to logic. It's time to have fun!

The purpose of this exercise is to loosen up the hard rock of habitual thought that stands between you and your idea reservoir. Trust in the process. Don't give up if the ideas don't come as quickly as you would like. Each time you try this exercise you'll dig further and further down toward your creative self. That's where you'll connect with the source of ideas.

And then one fine day soon there will be nothing between you and your idea reservoir. You'll be able to access it at anytime and anywhere you choose. Then you'll know you're on the path of the Creative Warrior.

26 Imagine New Uses for a Shoe

Do you the classic movie *Brazil?* There was a fantastic scene where the society ladies walk around the party with hats on their heads shaped like shoes? I still chuckle when I think about it. The funny thing was that the hats didn't look anything at all like normal looking hats. They just looked like big upside down footwear.

How did the writer come up with such a creative use for a shoe? Everyone knows that shoes are meant to be worn on your feet. Well that's what they are designed for anyway. But when we want to come up with new ideas we must forget convention. We must ignore what we've been taught about how things are meant to be used and imagine new uses for them.

For example, a shoe has a convenient shape for things other than feet. Add dirt and make it a planter. Add milk and use it as a cup. (Yuck!) Add garbage and use it as a small trash can. A few more creative ideas would be a door stop, puppy bed, and hand warmer.

By disregarding the function an object was designed for, we allow ourselves to see it in a different light. The world we thought we knew opens up. There's no right, there's no wrong. It's just you and your many ideas.

27 Count the Cereal Boxes

Did you know there are over 270,000 types of flowers in the world? Of just tulips, there are more than 3,700 registered varieties. Who knew?

And it's not just a multitude of flowers that the world has produced for us. There are 20,000 species of trees. 10,000 different types of birds. And, are you sitting down? There are over 1,000,000 varieties of insects in the world. That's a whole lot of creepy-looking, six-legged buggy things crawling around.

Variety is all around us. Take a road trip and survey how many different cars you see. There are over 60 car manufacturers producing an average of 20 different models each year. Do the math. Visit any store and start counting. At my local supermarket I once discovered over 250 types of cereal. It's a fact that people like variety.

Idea generation can be seen in a similar light. Okay you've come up with an idea. Don't stop there. Convince yourself that there are more, many more ideas, waiting to be discovered. Don't be disappointed when you realize that some ideas are a variation of the original concept. That's fine. After all, there's no substantial difference between Crispix and Chex cereals, but I'm very pleased that they both exist for my choosing.

28 Transform a Coffee Cup

In this manmade world of ours things are designed to accommodate the human form. For example, a coffee cup is sized so that we can hold it with one hand. Chairs are an appropriate height to allow us to sit without our feet dangling off the ground. The objects which we manufacture are first conceived with the end user in mind. We buy things that work for us. We wouldn't want it any other way. Or would we?

When it comes to creativity we need to remove our rational thinking caps. We must force ourselves to break away from the way things are and move towards the way things could be. Let's go back to our standard coffee cup. Can we come up with different cup designs?

A cup could be square, oval or baton-shaped. It could as big as a milk container or as small as a thimble. The opening could be in the middle or the bottom. Now you may be thinking that a coffee cup with an opening in the bottom is not going to work. And of course you'd be right. Until you start to think about how to cap the opening. Maybe there's a way to design the cap so that you don't even need to pick up the cup to drink. With some out-of-the-box thinking I'm sure you could make your idea work.

However this book is not about designing but about generating ideas. If we didn't allow ourselves to transform 'what is' into 'what could be', then we'd go nowhere. Things are the way they are for good reasons. But that doesn't mean we should stop ourselves from

exploring alternative ways. Creative Warriors know that
new ideas are built on the solid foundation of what has
already been done.

29 Respect Your Socks

Socks don't get the respect they deserve. Typically they're hidden all day under the overwhelming presence of pants. Hence they don't get much attention when it comes time to choosing which pair to wear.

Why not try something new today? Instead of choosing socks to blend in with your pants, let them stand out. How about a bright citrus green against a navy blue pant leg? Now you're having fun. What else, besides raising a few eyebrows, would this achieve?

By focusing on your sock selection, you start your day by rattling your brain in a thoughtful, energized way. You're autopilot switch doesn't kick in because you are in tune with what you're actually doing. Thoughts begin to flow. Ideas form. Creativity awakens. What started at your feet may just go to your head.

30 Imagine Corn Growing on a Tree

We think in concepts based on the things we've experienced. For example, we know what a tree is supposed to look like and we recognize one when we see it.

We all know a tree has a trunk, branches and leaves. This is the picture we carry around in our heads. However we have the option to change that picture at any time for no particular reason.

Now imagine a tree growing ears of corn instead of leaves. Why stop there? Imagine shoes instead of leaves. How about boxes of cereal. Trees can inspire brainstorming. Imagine anything you want up there. It doesn't need to make sense.

Mix it up. Loosen up. Have fun. This is how creativity starts. Logic and rational thought are fine when you want to create a plan and take action. Imagination and intuition are what you'll need to see the world differently and generate new ideas.

31 Get In Touch with Your Stapler

I'd like you to think back to when you were a kid sitting in your backyard right after sunset. Staring up at the darkening sky you were filled with a sense of wonder. Your thoughts strayed to far-flung adventures. Riding on the tail of a comet. Walking on the sun. Hopping on surface of the Moon. Ahh, the good old days.

Those times were magical because in your kid mind everything was possible. Your imagination was wide open. The line between reality and fantasy was either blurry or non-existent. You were a carefree soul riding along on the wings of time. No worries about the future. No regrets concerning the past.

What if we could bring a little of that carefree attitude into our adult lives? Is it possible to forget about planning for tomorrow and live in the moment? I'm not suggesting doing this all day. We all have our adult responsibilities. However, there are moments in everyone's busy lives when it makes sense to take a break.

For example, you've just finished an important task you've been feverishly working on for most of the day. You've just hit the send button and it's done. Now what? Do you immediately jump into your next task? Wouldn't it make sense to relax for a couple of minutes? Stop working and give yourself a break. A total and complete break. Is this even possible? Of course it is.

You can decouple from your thoughts at any time. It's not as hard as you may think. It'll take some practice like anything else that's worth doing in life. There are many methods. The technique I'm going to show you is particularly useful when you don't have much time and don't feel like moving away from your desk.

The first thing to do is to convince yourself that you truly want to take a break. Give yourself a goal. For example, tell yourself that you will not entertain any thoughts for the next five minutes. Do this with conviction. A half-hearted wish will just not do. You have to really want it.

Now that you've convinced yourself that you need to take a break from your thoughts, it's time to actually do it. The key here is to focus on the physical world immediately around you. Whatever you can see is what you should be focusing on. And everything is fair game. If you choose to focus on your pen, that's fine. If you want to focus on your computer screen, that's okay too. But make sure it's turned off. The changing images on the screen will be distracting.

Focus on the object you've chosen. With your eyes only, trace the object's outline. Follow its curves and angles. Move slowly and really feel the object with your eyes. Explore its weight, color and texture. Compare it to other objects around it. For example, which object is heavier, the pen or the staple remover? If the pen is blue, compare it to the color of the sky today. Don't close your eyes and imagine, but open your eyes and see. The point of this exercise is to connect directly with the world without thinking abstractly about it.

Focusing on the objects around you takes you out of your own head. You are not in some abstract imaginary place, but experiencing the here and now. How does this exercise help you to be more creative? You'll find that reconnecting with the present moment is highly energizing. In addition, your reality can be just as inspiring for creative thinking as your imagination. There's much to explore out there. The ordinary world can be a fascinating place when we choose to focus on what's in front of us.

32 Seek out the Gray

The world can be understood as consisting of many sets of opposites. Night opposes day, winter sits at the opposite end from summer. The list goes on and on. A dualistic perspective is how we have been taught to see reality.

In order to communicate effectively we need to share a conceptual framework with others. This common understanding is necessary for language to work. However, it is not how creativity works.

Dualistic thinking inhibits creativity. We need to see past the idea that the world merely consists of opposites. Creativity is about seeing possibilities and alternatives. We must wipe our minds clean of dualism. How can we do this?

One approach is to remind ourselves that there are an infinite number of points between the opposite ends of the dualistic spectrum. For example, think about all the shades of gray between the black and white. In a real sense there is no limit. This type of thinking will help break down our conceptual dams and allow our creativity to flow freely.

33 Ask "What if" a Lot

Knowing things feels good. For example, when I open up a container of milk and begin to pour, I know the milk will plummet into my bowl of cereal. I know this because it did the same thing yesterday and the day before. In fact, my milk has always performed this way. Before we learn about the law of gravity in school, we know that milk will always travel downward when poured.

What would happen if one sunny morning the law of gravity ceased to exist? That's right, all of a sudden without any warning milk started acting really weird. In this zero gravity environment not only the milk but our bodies would be drifting upward. Beyond that it's anyone's guess as to what would occur. Would the milk and the bowl be moving upwards at the same rate of speed? Would they both stop moving eventually? Does milk at zero gravity stay in a continuous stream or transform into droplets? If we turn the bowl upside-down and place it above the milk, would we be able to capture the milk in it?

The questions can go on and on. And that's precisely my point. Since we don't know for sure what would happen within this new scenario, we are free of the conceptual boundaries that typically constrain us. Possibilities open up to us and, instead of seeing what is, we see what could be. It's quite liberating. However, do we need to wait until a major law of the universe drops away to begin to open our minds? Of course not. We can do it any time we want.

Einstein called this type of thinking 'thought experiments'. He famously imagined himself running alongside a beam of light. He constructed the scene in his head and imagined what would happen if he ran at the speed of light. It didn't matter to Einstein that he would never be able to physically experience what he was imagining. All that mattered was that in the mind of Einstein it made sense. His conclusion was the basis for his Special Theory of Relativity, which would completely change how we understand our world.

To usher in a creative mindset you need to get comfortable with not knowing. You must use your imagination to fill in the blanks. Try asking yourself : what would happen if this took place. The key to that last thought is the word "if." That's the concept that allows you to discover novel possibilities. It lets you see the world in ways you have never seen it before. 'If' frees you from habitual thinking and lets you see things anew.

When conducting a thought experiment, don't force the results. Don't try to control what happens. Just let the actions unfold. You are on a journey of discovery. Relax and let go. Don't analyze or evaluate your moves. Remind yourself that you really don't know where this experiment will end up. Open your mind to new experiences. It's your ticket to becoming a Creative Warrior.

34 Don't Lose Your Mind

Listening to the sounds of nature can be very calming.
The peaceful gurgling of a brook. The soft whoosh of
the wind through pine trees. These sounds help you
focus your mind on the soothing experiences of the
present moment.

However, we aren't always taking a leisurely walk in the
woods. Most of our time is spent in environments that
aren't peaceful at all. The stress of the office; the
hurried pace of doing errands on the weekend; the
hours spent sitting in traffic. Can we become centered
in these energized situations? Yes we can.

The key is to focus our distracted minds. It doesn't
matter what we choose to concentrate on as long as we
don't give up at the first sign of adversity. When
random thoughts pull you away, simply bring your
mind back to the thing you chose to focus on. I prefer
to concentrate on a sound, though an object or smell
could work just as well.

The important thing to remember is when your mind
wanders, and it undoubtedly will, simply bring it back
to your object of concentration. Do not blame or
chastise yourself. Do not judge yourself at all. Treat
yourself with respect.

Try this exercise next time you want to give your
creativity a boost. It works because it helps you to
become focused on the present moment. That's where
your creativity lives.

35 Learn from a Rock

"That's ridiculous, what can a rock teach me?" might be the initial thought that runs through your mind. Well, I'm here to tell you how a lowly rock can help you find your creativity.

Logically a rock shouldn't be able to teach us anything. Yes that's true. But logic is not the only way to see. Keep an open mind. Go in to yourself and let your imagination take flight. You'll need to let your thoughts flow freely no matter how ridiculous they may seem at first.

The rock won't start talking to you. But if you look at it, really focus on it, your mind may begin to percolate with ideas. This particular rock may bring up thoughts of sitting on a beach with your parents or playing a game with your friends. You may associate that game with a song whose lyrics remind you of feelings you've long forgotten. Those feelings may lead to thoughts you had as a kid which then helps you to see your current situation in a new light. Go with the flow of ideas and who knows where you may end up.

36 Leave Home at a Different Time

Wake up, brush teeth, get dressed, eat breakfast, go to work, come home, eat dinner, watch TV and go to sleep. Repeat each day. Does your life sometimes remind you of the movie *Groundhog Day*?

We tend to do the same things in the same way, day after day. We do things this way because we're creatures of habit. We like to feel comfortable and know what to expect. Who needs surprises anyway?

What would happen if you deliberately changed something in your routine in some small way? For example, try leaving home fifteen minutes earlier than you typically do. You may find yourself in a radically different situation. You may meet someone new on the train platform. You may hear a new program on the radio. You may sit in a new seat and see new sights along the way.

Little changes can push us towards new experiences. What a difference fifteen minutes can do for your creative potential. Get out of your comfort zone and try it today.

37 Talk Nonsense

College students have been known to do some very
outlandish things. I was no exception. While a
freshman in the artsy East Village of NYC, I'd see all
sorts of bohemians doing all sorts of interesting things.
Did they influence my behavior? Sure did.

One memorable day my roommate and I were walking
out of our favorite bar when we started to slur a few
words. No surprise there. On this particular afternoon
we took pleasure upon hearing the funny sounds we
were making. We got to our apartment and found
ourselves still slurring. Though sober now, we
continued slurring through dinner. We went to sleep
and the slurring went on through the wall between our
bedrooms.

The next day we were back to our normal selves, but
decided to continue the silliness of the previous day. It
was still very funny. We created a name for our slurred
language: Schluz. During the next three years of school
Schluz travelled with us. Whenever we needed a break
from studying we spoke it. If we wanted to goof on a
stranger we spoke it. If we needed a laugh we spoke it.
We used Schluz any time we felt that we were getting
too serious.

Little did anyone listening to us know that Schulz was a
nonsense language. It had no literal meaning. We just
liked the way it sounded and we were making it up on
the fly. It loosened us up. We were flowing along in our
stream of consciousness wackiness. It felt very

liberating. It helped to free ourselves of our habitual thinking. I believe that was the biggest reason we talked Schluz. New ways of seeing. New ways of thinking. We were well on our way to becoming Creative Warriors.

38 Take Off Your Glasses

If you've worn glasses for any length of time you probably don't even notice them anymore. You put them on in the morning and you see clearly through the day. They do their job well. They've become part of you.

Did you know that when your glasses are off your other senses are heightened? That's right. You become aware of sounds you never would have heard with your glasses on. Odors that didn't register before now come to the forefront of your consciousness. All because you took your glasses off.

The principle works in other ways as well. Put ear muffs on and you'll find that your sense of sight is more acute. You see details that you'd ordinarily pass right over. Colors become more vivid. You feel the firmness or softness of the ground you're walking on. All because you put your ear muffs on.

The way you experience your surroundings is not fixed. Alter any one of your senses and a whole new world will open up for you. New sensations lead to new perceptions which can lead to new thoughts and ideas. Creativity here we come.

39 Watch a River

I enjoy sitting on the banks of a river. The movement of the water is beautiful to watch. What I don't appreciate is a dam in the river. There's something sad about a river that has stopped flowing. It's in a river's nature to move and continue its journey downstream.

A flowing river is analogous to the movement of your creativity. Think of your ideas as leaves in the water. Rocks are the obstacles that may snag the leaves. If there are no rocks then the leaves will continue downstream unimpeded. Similarly if there are no obstacles in your stream of consciousness then your ideas will flow smoothly.

The number one obstacle preventing your creativity from flowing is criticism before its appropriate time. A thought such as "this is a bad idea" will kill any idea immediately. The cure...just don't do it. Let that negative thought go. Instead try convincing yourself that ideas are dynamic. They shift, change and morph as time goes by. A bad idea may turn into a good one if you don't let your judging mind get in the way.

It's hard to suspend judgment. We've been taught that we must be efficient in our thinking. Bad ideas are a waste of time. Don't believe the hype. In fact, when it comes to creativity nothing could be further from the truth. You'll be rewarded if you let your river of ideas flow deep and wide.

40 Take a Break

Have you ever spent time concentrating on a problem and felt that the solution was just out of reach? It's the same type of feeling as when you see someone and can't remember his or her name: It's on the tip of my tongue. You try to reel it in but it refuses to budge.

This is all part of the creative process. Inspiration rarely arrives without a struggle. Even creative geniuses like Thomas Edison had this experience. He had a solution (of course). He would take break from what he was doing, climb up on his work table and take a power nap.

Edison would neither be asleep nor fully awake. He'd put his mind in a state of flux akin to a daydream. He'd let his thoughts wander through his subconscious. No grasping after ideas. No impediments to his creative flow.

After 10 minutes or so he'd get up from his table and begin to work on the problem that had been just out of reach moments earlier. More often than not an answer would soon pop into his conscious mind.

This may sound like magic to you, but not to Edison. He knew that while he was napping his subconscious mind was working. He taught himself a way to let his creative process keep moving.

Now it's your turn. Don't give up if it doesn't work the first time. The key is to let your mind relax. Give up all control. It may feel uncomfortable but in time it will become second nature. Then this technique will become a tool in your Creative Warrior toolbox.

41 Watch Television with the Sound Off

TV is a medium composed of pictures and noise. What would happen if we watched with the sound off? Would we still understand the messages the characters were trying to convey?

True communication is both verbal and non-verbal. Verbal consists of words and language. Non-verbal includes gestures and body language. Research has shown that 70% of all meaning is derived via non-verbal means. This tells us that if an actor is effectively using his body to support his words then we won't get lost when we watch without the sound.

Watching TV this way can help us to become more creative. How? Watching without the benefit of dialog encourages us to get in touch with our bodies in order to understand what's happening on the screen. When we are in contact with our feelings and emotions we become more sensitive to ourselves and the world around us. It's not about zoning out. It's about tuning in.

42 Move Slower

Our lives are busy. We're always on the go. We can't afford to forget what needs to be done so we create lists. We try to complete our lists as quickly as possible. We feel good as we check off each item.

Our lists keep us moving around our home and our office and our town with purpose. We go through our lists quickly so we can give ourselves more time to do what we really want to do. Unfortunately by the time we're finished with our lists, we're too tired to do anything else.

Moving at our top speed may get us to our destinations quickly; however a slower pace will lead to less stress. Being relaxed allows us to open our eyes and ears. We experience things previously passed over while we were rushing around. We put ourselves in the frame of mind to do things in new ways.

The path of the Creative Warrior is not necessarily straight. Twists and turns may take us to places we've never been. We're on a journey of discovery. Move slower and enjoy it.

43 Listen for the Subtle Whisper of an Idea

You may be asking yourself: how can I listen to something that doesn't exist? Non-physical objects do make sounds. Ask a musician, he'll tell you all about it.

From classical to jazz to rock to hip-hop, all these musical formats have something significant in common...the silence that exists between the notes. I'm not talking philosophy here. Put in your ear buds and listen to your favorite song. Turn up the volume higher than you typically would. Find the spot where the music stops completely. It may occur for only a moment so listen closely. Now pause your music player.

Did you hear it? Softer than a whisper, but it was there. Silence exists because of sound. It takes sensitivity to hear silence. Out of silence come thoughts and ideas. A Creative Warrior knows it takes sensitivity to hear the subtle whisper of an idea being born.

44 Take a Walk in the Rain

"Why would I take a walk in the rain? I'll get wet" is a common response to that suggestion. Sure you'll get wet. Sure you may feel uncomfortable at first. The real issue is whether you can embrace the new situation and move out of your comfort zone.

I'm not suggesting that you do this activity in a monsoon. Wait for a gentle summer rain. Take an umbrella if there's a chance of a heavy downpour. There's no reason to be anxious. That would defeat the purpose of your stroll.

Your goal is to open yourself up to new sensations. Feel the water on your skin. Listen to the rhythm of the raindrops as they hit the leaves around you. Smell the air as it's cleansed by the rain. Open up.

Relax and focus on the sights and sounds around you. Lose your sense of time. Stay present. Soon you may stumble upon the path of the Creative Warrior.

45 The Power of Alternative Thinking

Math is wonderful. It allows us to use a non-verbal language to describe objects and phenomena in clear and precise ways. Math leaves us with the impression that the world is full of answers. 1+1=2. Parallel lines never meet. A square has four sides. Math is indeed powerful. If you think in mathematical terms, then there is only one answer to every question. You've entered a world with no room for error.

I'm not knocking math, but the creative mind is not fond of absolutes. If you think there is only one way to do something, you'll find yourself up against a wall very quickly.

Next time you are looking for inspiration, try using words such as: and, also, or. Creative Warriors understand that these are the words which will permit their minds to generate multiple ideas to the same problem.

46 Ride the Wind

Have you ever been stuck with an unwanted thought?
You ignore it, but it pops back in. You swap it for a
new thought, but it pushes its way back. It just won't
go away no matter how hard you try.

What's the problem here? Usually the harder we try, the
more successful we are. Not in this case. The harder we
try to push a thought away, the harder it pushes back.
That's just the way the mind works. No amount of
effort will change that fact. What to do?

Instead of pushing the thought away, don't do
anything. Leave it alone and pay it no attention. Give it
no energy. Visualize a wind flowing through your head
carrying the thought away with it.

This technique works to remove unwanted thoughts
from your mind. It also works to usher in new thoughts
because the mind abhors a vacuum. Try it when you
need a creative boost.

47 Ponder the Stars

The night sky is amazing. There are stars everywhere you look. Some astronomers claim there are 400 billion stars in our Milky Way Galaxy. Multiply that number by the 100 billion or so galaxies in the universe. WOW! it gets you thinking about the enormity of our universe.

This line of thought may eventually lead to the idea of how small you are in relationship to everything. If you get to this point, don't turn it into a negative, depressing thought. Stay upbeat and think about how much more there is for you to explore and learn.

Open yourself up to the fact that the potential for knowledge is huge. The world is brimming with ideas. It's an enormous untapped creative gold mine just waiting for you.

48 Get Lost in the Web

Each time I surf the internet I'm amazed at how much information it contains. With a few clicks of my mouse, I can find anything I'm looking for.

The fun part for me is that during my searches I also find things I wasn't looking for. I often veer off course and become lost in the immense information highway.

Many people would call this getting distracted. Not productive, nor efficient. I think the process of getting lost is my destination. It opens me up to different ways of thinking and new ideas. My mind enjoys moving smoothly within the flow of ideas.

Getting lost in the web can open you up to a new world. It ushers in the right attitude to consider possibilities that you may have previously rejected with a tighter mind set. Exploring the internet will surely help your creative juices to flow.

49 Taste Some Juicy Half Baked Ideas

An effective technique to facilitate the flow of ideas is called brainstorming. This is how it works... one problem is selected for group discussion. The participants offer up their ideas as soon as they come to mind. Any idea will do. A scribe collects all of the ideas without ranking or categorizing them.

Sounds easy, doesn't it? Try it and see what happens. You may notice that you feel something holding you back from freely offering up your ideas during the brainstorming session. This can be attributed to the strong urge to evaluate the correctness of your idea BEFORE offering it to the group.

Why do we do this when the rules of brainstorming say any idea will do? The reason is that we don't want to offer a half-baked idea to the group. We imagine that it will make us look dumb.

To encourage the flow of creativity, we must get over the idea that all ideas must be good ones. The point is to let your ideas go without pre-judging them. You can evaluate the value and relevancy of your ideas AFTER you unleash them into the world.

50 Step Away from the Heat

Imagine this scenario: You're having a discussion with a good friend. The topic is something casual like the weather. You come to a point where you see things differently and the conversation gets heated. You feel that you are right and want to prove your point. Your friend is not giving in. You dig in harder. You argue and get angry at each other. You and your friend manage to walk away from the discussion, but not on very good terms.

What happened? How could two close friends get so mad at each other over a seemingly trivial issue? Unfortunately it happens all the time. We get so wrapped up in our own point of view that we forget that our friend believes his or her opinion is just as valid as ours.

The more we do this, the harder it is to see a different perspective. We often forget that we have a choice: dig in or step back. Digging in will make you get defensive and close-minded. Stepping back will allow you to be flexible and see the world in a different way. The latter one is the path of the Creative Warrior.

51 Make an Intentional Mistake

It's fun to discover new ways of seeing the world. It's our birthright as humans to learn new things. That's how we grow intellectually and emotionally.

Learning provides us with knowledge we didn't have previously. Sometimes we learn by reading books. Other times we learn by doing. And there are times when we learn as a consequence of making a mistake.

I just heard a collective gasp from my readers. It's okay; mistakes are a part of life. If we're afraid to make a mistake, then it follows that we have a fear of learning. New ideas are bound to lead us to mistakes. That's just natural.

We must embrace the fact that we WILL make mistakes. That's how creativity works. Are you brave enough to make a mistake intentionally? Try it. It will help you to remember this: making a mistake happens once, but the gain in knowledge will last a lifetime.

52 Start Walking

There's so much to explore in this big country of ours. You can spend your whole life traveling and still not see it all. However, there's much to experience closer to home.

You can find your creativity anywhere. All you need to do is take a short trip. You don't need to plan it out. Anywhere will do because the destination isn't as important as the journey. In fact, I suggest you take it one step further and not even think about a destination.

Step out your door and start walking. Just go. Don't think about direction. Don't think about schedule. Just go where your legs want to take you and keep on moving. You'll be amazed at how much more there is to see when you're not trying to be somewhere by a specific time. Even if you've traveled this route many times you'll notice things you weren't aware of when you were rushing to get somewhere.

Your journey will lead to new sights and sounds which will lead to new thoughts and ideas. You've just opened the floodgates of creativity by taking a simple walk around town.

53 Dash to the New

There are two types of people in the world...those who enjoy being creative and those who enjoy following a routine. There are pros and cons to both tendencies. Depending on the circumstance, a person who is generally creative may choose to go with routine-based behavior or vice versa.

In the interest of self-awareness, it's important to understand your dominant and subdominant tendencies. Learning about yourself helps you to grow as a person. With this in mind, I've created two lists that will assist you in recognizing where you lie on the creativity spectrum.

List A

I consistently try new ways of doing things because:

1) I enjoy the feeling of exploration and discovery

2) I like having new sensations and experiences

3) I think being creative is its own reward

4) I feel energized when a new idea arrives

5) I find doing this leads me to innovative ideas and new ways of seeing

6) I get bored easily

List B

I typically do things the same way because:

1) I don't enjoy surprises

2) I find that it's worked in the past

3) I like to know what to expect

4) I don't want to waste time re-inventing the wheel

5) I know I won't fail

6) I'm a creature of habit

Which list resonated more with you, A or B? There is no right answer. Each of us goes back and forth between being creative (list A) and habitual (list B). We can use these lists if we choose to move towards the opposite of our natural tendency. Some people feel they have an excess of creativity. However, I'd suspect that if you are reading this book you are interested in becoming more creative.

Creativity is all about getting to the new. New what? New anything...new sensations, new perceptions, new thoughts and new ideas. It's about opening yourself up to new experiences, giving yourself new opportunities and moving yourself out of your comfort zone. It can be scary, exhilarating and energizing, all at the same time. There may be some failure mixed in. That's okay because that's how we learn. Go ahead and try something new today. Creativity awaits you.

54 Use Your Bad Mood for Good

Sometimes we wake up in a grumpy mood. Maybe it was caused by a bad dream. Maybe it carried over from a negative incident during the day before. Whatever the reason we all can agree that it's not a good way to begin your day. Or is it?

A negative mindset can color our daily perceptions. However, that situation is not necessarily a bad thing. A negative mood may cause us to see and think about the world in different ways than we normally do. Any time we experience the world in new ways, we give our creativity a chance to blossom.

Now I'm not advocating intentionally cultivating a bad mood. But if you find yourself in a mindset that doesn't feel quite right don't immediately freak out. Relax, accept it, and see where it leads. Ideas that you'd normally ignore, reject or suppress may bubble up to the surface of your mind and inspire you. Learn to see your down mood as an opportunity to think differently and you'll be on the road to becoming a Creative Warrior.

55 Be a Scatter Brain

This morning I feel a bit tired. Last night I stayed up two hour later than usual and now I'm paying for it. My body says I need a minimum of seven hours of sleep. Five or six is just not enough.

I like to start my day by reading the newspaper. My head is hungry for information. Today my head is not very hungry. It just wants to be left alone to meander where it wants to go. My head is not interested in focusing on anything in particular. It's content just to be.

We're taught that we should always be doing something, anything. An idle mind is the devil's playground. You can rest when you are dead. No rest for the weary. These are some of the sentiments we hear. How can an unfocused mind be anything but bad for us?

When it comes to creativity, being scatterbrained can be a very good thing. The word 'scatterbrained' carries a negative connotation. However when you analyze the word you'll see that a primary component is "scatter". One of the definitions of this word is: throw in various random directions. What good can possibly come from treating your brain in such a manner? The key is to understand that the way to generate ideas, many ideas, is to do just what the definition refers to...throw your mind in various random directions.

Imagine you hold many small pebbles. Now scatter them and see how they've landed all over the place.

Various random directions. You may be thinking that those are just pebbles, not your mind. And in any case you have only one mind. You can't scatter something that's whole.

Well I'm here to tell you that that thought is holding you back from reaching your creative potential. You may conceive of your mind as a thing, but it's not. It's not because your mind is not a physical object. Your brain is physical, your mind is not. So it follows that your mind can in be scattered in many various directions.

What does this mean? Try different ways of doing things. Don't let yourself get bogged down with ideas of how the world 'should' work. Let your mind work with contradictory ideas. Squint rather than stare. Take the path less taken. Be light on your feet. Let the world's mysteries remain mysterious. That's the way of the Creative Warrior.

56 Get to Know the *Mona Lisa*

In my humble opinion, the painting by Leonardo daVinci called the *Mona Lisa* is one of the world's finest works of art. I would not say that she is a classically beautiful woman like Vermeer's *Girl with a Pearl Earring*. Nor is she stunningly beautiful like Botticelli's *Venus*. However, she does have a certain something going for her that the other women portrayed do not...her enigmatic smile.

Without that smile she'd be just another face in the crowd. The way she subtlety turns up the left side of her mouth captures the viewer's attention like no other woman. Study her. I bet she stirs up your imagination. What's she thinking? Is she happy? Did she just do something devious? Is she planning to do something pleasurable? What's she hiding behind that smile? So very intriguing.

Thinking about the *Mona Lisa* will jump start your creativity. She makes you ask yourself questions which can't be answered definitively. That's because there is no one right answer. She keeps you guessing. Your mind becomes receptive to endless possibilities. Once you capture that feeling of openness, stay with it. Keep it going. That's the attitude you'll need to become a Creative Warrior.

57 Wear Your Hat Backwards

When I was in high school I'd roam the halls with a big cowboy hat on. Why? It made me feel unique. Then the trend started to catch on and it seemed like everyone wanted to look like a cowboy. I stopped wearing a hat and looked for something new to do.

When I look back on those days I understand what was driving me to do it. Sure it made me feel special by calling attention to myself. But there was something else. Something more than ego that was motivating me. Wearing a hat was not something I did every day. Maybe once or twice a week. Those special days felt different not only because I stood out, but because it made me see the world differently. How does this work?

We all have a daily routine. We more or less do the same things each day. We get out of bed on the same side each morning. We get our coffee from the same shop each morning. We take the same train each morning. We start checking our emails the same time each morning. There's nothing wrong with our habits; it's just the way we do things. We feel comfortable knowing what to expect from our environment, from ourselves and from others we interact with.

When we introduce a new variable into our routine, like wearing a big hat, a small shift occurs which can have big implications for the way we do things. Our minds react to something new by turning off our auto-pilot switch. Our senses are heightened and we become more aware of our surroundings. We begin to notice things that had previously slipped under our radar. We react to new stimulus in unpredictable ways. That's a good thing because it gets us thinking and subsequently acting in new and creative directions.

This is what happens when we break our routine and act differently. However, the change does not have to be as outrageous as wearing a big cowboy hat. For example, it could be as minor as wearing the hat you typically wear backwards. Try it, see how it feels. It may take you slightly out of your comfort zone. And that's exactly where you want to be when your goal is to become a Creative Warrior.

58 Let Your Nose Lead the Way

Have you ever found yourself in a foreign city without a map? In these days of cell phones and GPS it's almost impossible to get lost. However, if it's your intent to get lost you can very easily do it. Just turn off your phone.

After getting over the initial anxiety, you may find this technique exhilarating. No longer focused on where you're going you'll be free to explore where you are. It's quite possible that you'll choose to let your nose lead the way. You may follow the first scent you detect and it may take you to a shop with oven fresh pastries. Or maybe you'll hear something interesting and discover to an incredible band.

Along the way there may be other interesting sights and sounds that make you stop. You could get engrossed in a conversation with a friendly stranger. Or a funky hotel lobby may pull you in. Everything is fair game as you allow yourself to lose control and take in the sights and sounds of where you are. Let the new experiences lead to new ideas. Your nose knows.

59 Go Zip Lining

Hanging from a thin cord and moving at speeds close to 50 mph while your feet are dangling inches above the highest tree is thrilling. Watching everything zip past you in a blur is an exciting experience. Nothing can stop you. Wow!

Does that sound like fun to you? No? Well you're not alone. Many people don't include this activity on top of their summer vacation to do list. Thinking about zip lining can be scary. We're not used to flying through the air. We're not used to moving so fast. We're not accustomed to seeing things whizz by us. We don't enjoy being out of control.

My first zip line experience was no different. I felt nauseous waiting my turn on the zip line tower. Watching people speed through the air and come back to earth jazzed up and laughing didn't help me feel any better. I had knots in my stomach and found it hard to breathe. Every 30 seconds I'd hear that inner voice urging me to turn around and get back to safe solid ground. Every muscle in my body was dead set against me. Yet I didn't quit. I knew that if I did I'd never have the chance again.

In the end I worked through my fear. In fact, I enjoyed the thrilling sensations so much that I went back for another ride. I accomplished what I set out to do. But something else happened that day that was totally unexpected.

All throughout the day I was thinking about a problem I had been working on before leaving for vacation. I know, I know, on vacation you're supposed to leave your work issues behind. Well somehow they jumped into my suitcase while I wasn't looking. In any case, on the ride back to the hotel after zip lining, I remembered how the landscape appeared as it flew past me below: a fantastic cacophony of lines, shapes and color. My mind associated that mosaic image with an idea about synergy that led me towards a solution to my work dilemma. Without the zip line experience I don't believe I would ever have solved the problem in the way I did that day.

Now I keep a picture of the zip line tower at my desk. I often use it as inspiration when I'm stuck. Looking at it relaxes me and frees my mind to think in new directions. In addition, it feels good to remember the moment I overcame my fear and moved onto the path of the Creative Warrior.

60 Watch Classic Music Videos

I am a member of the MTV generation. I remember the day it started like it was yesterday: August 1, 1981. All of my friends huddled around our 19" TV watching the first music video in history: Video Killed the Radio Star by The Buggles. It was a funky black and white video of a bespeckled man lamenting over the fall of the radio singers to the newly appointed video music stars. How appropriate.

This memory is still fresh in my mind. I remember the weather, the food and my friends' punk-wannabe hair styles. I remember the look and feel of the apartment I shared with my two roommates. It's as if the thirty year old event happened no more than thirty days ago.

These memories are vigorously stirred up every time I watch The Buggles video. When I explore the sights and sounds of that memory I find a treasure trove of material to work with. Old thoughts and feelings intermingle and meld with my present thinking. And VOILA! something completely new is born.

Next time you're stuck, turn on MTV or You Tube and watch classic videos. Relive long forgotten experiences. Connect with your past. By kicking up the dusty memories you may just find some shiny new ideas.

61 Give a Speech at a Toastmasters Club

Most people are more afraid of speaking in front of an audience than they are of dying. That's a curious fact. What makes it so scary to speak in front of a group of people? We may be afraid that we'll look stupid. Maybe we don't like the feeling of being in the spotlight. Some of us may feel paralyzed by perfectionism. There are many reasons for people to fear the stage.

If you want to overcome your fear of public speaking then joining a Toastmasters club is for you. Each meeting is structured to allow 3 or 4 people to each speak for 5 to 7 minutes. These types of speeches are called prepared speeches. The participants write their speeches prior to coming to the club to present them. The content of the speech can be about anything, but each speech is focused on a different topic. Vocal intonation, body language and speech structure are a few of the issues you'll work on.

Standing on stage in front of an audience does not come natural to many people. However, the more you do it, the easier it becomes. You begin to realize that you don't need to memorize your speech word for word. You begin to trust yourself and let the flow of the moment take over. The members of the audience don't know what you're going to say before you say it. Only you do. So you can say anything you want in any style you choose. It's up to you on whether you will meander a bit. It's up to if you want to tell a story. It's up to you if you want to inject some humor into your speech. It's your choice because you're the only one on stage. You own the moment.

This technique can become one of your favorites. It offers an opportunity to be break free from a mind that is preoccupied with the 'right' way to do things. Public speaking makes you realize that there are numerous ways to do the same thing. Each speaker is different. Each speech is unique. The key is not to stop after your initial speech. Continue on your path and your fear of the stage will dissipate. You'll actually look forward to speaking because a Creative Warrior knows that creativity lives on the cutting edge of the present moment.

62 Enjoy the Journey

By now I'm sure you've found a few Creative Warrior techniques that work for you. Many of them encourage you to put yourself in situations that are a bit out of your comfort zone. Here you will learn various things about yourself. Trust in your capacity to handle the unexpected is one big benefit. As you continue on your quest you'll realize that there is no right way to handle the situations you'll find yourself in. There are many opinions on how to do something. The choice is always yours.

You'll realize that the outcome is not as important as the process. You may have goals in mind when using the techniques. If you don't achieve them, no big deal. It's what you've learned during your adventure that counts. It's beneficial to take notes after each attempt. Jot down where you felt out of your comfort zone and how you chose to act. Read the notes before you go on your next adventure.

You may feel the urge to berate yourself for feeling a bit anxious or unsure of yourself. This is only natural. In time, those feelings will be replaced by a sense of excitement and confidence. Accelerate this process by choosing to trust your instincts and listening to your intuition.

Don't take yourself too seriously when brainstorming. Remember how you felt as a child. You were on a journey of discovery. The fun part was playing around with ideas. You were not afraid to challenge yourself with "what if" and "how come." These were the type of questions that breathed life into your creative playtime.

Life becomes joyful when you realize that the present moment provides you with continuous opportunities to explore, learn and grow. Being at ease in the moment is the key to helping you to see the world with fresh eyes and to think with an open mind. Stay on this path and soon you will become the Creative Warrior you were meant to be.

63 Wrap Up

I hope you had fun working through the various techniques included in this book. Creativity is not a one shot deal. I encourage you use this book as a practical guide to develop your creative confidence. Remember that anything you do can be enhanced by bringing a Creative Warrior mindset to your activities.

The following eight principles are the foundation of that mindset:

1 Alternatives
Loosen up and see many possibilities. Convince yourself that there's more than one way to do/think/feel/say/see things.

2 Discovery
Put yourself in situations which can provide new experiences for you. Get out of your comfort zone.

3 Awareness
a. Don't do things out of habit; become aware of your actions.

b. Don't see things out of habit; become aware of the world around you.

c. Don't think things out of habit; become aware of the thoughts in your head. Give them respect.

4 Change
Go with the flow, don't try to control everything. Keep up with the dynamic scenario. Everything changes; so should you.

5 Learn
Don't worry about having to be right all the time. It's okay to make a mistake because that's how we learn new ways to do/think/feel/say/see.

6 Experiment
Don't be overly concerned about the end results of your actions. Imagine yourself on a journey. Enjoy what you are doing while you are doing it. Be in the moment.

7 Intuition
Rational thought is not the only way we understand the world. Learn to trust your inner voice. Your job is to energize your creative potential.

8 Play
Remember the sense of lightness you felt as a child. You don't need to be serious all the time. Relax, enjoy and have fun.

64 Your Thoughts

Don't let your good creative work go to waste. After practicing with each technique, jot down your ideas and insights on the following blank pages.

And please visit my website *CreativeWarriorSecrets.com* for additional simple yet powerful tips on developing creativity and achieving your peak performance.

I look forward to hearing from you on all of your successes as you progress on the path of the Creative Warrior. Have fun!